Seven Days in Heaven

Emmanuel Twagirimana

ISBN: 1-933899-53-0

Published by:
Holy Fire Publishing
Unit 116
1525-D Old Trolley Rd.
Summerville, SC 29485
www.ChristianPublish.com

Cover Design: Jay Cookingham

Printed in the United States of America and the United Kingdom

ACKNOWLEDGEMENTS

My deepest gratitude goes to The Almighty God, thank you for the gift of salvation.

To my Dear wife Isabelle, thank you for your endless love and support,

Dr John Simpson obeyed the Holy Spirit and came over to Kigali to treat me, a man he didn't know. I am grateful to him for taking the journey of faith that answered my prayer, in my greatest hour of need. His big heart changed my life.

To Bishop Dr Arthur Kitonga, for providing shelter and above all the love that nursed me back to health. He perceived the gift of God in me, and availed opportunities for my call to grow. You are more than a spiritual father, but a mentor and a friend.

Thanks to Brother Makko Musagara, Pastor David Githinji, Rev. Enoch Rubaduka and Mr. Silas Kanamugire for your support and wise counsel.

Last, but not the least, to Rev Dennis Walker, Michael Wambugu and Mona L. Nduilu, whose hard work and professionalism made it possible for this book to be published.

DEDICATION

To my lovely kids Joshua and
Jemima, great gifts from The
Lord.

FOREWARD

During the 1994 war in Rwanda, Emmanuel was injured by pieces of shrapnel from a bomb that hit his neighbour's house. He later died and came back to life after seven days. Emmanuel thought he was gone just for hours but not so - those who witnessed the killing attested that he'd been dead for 7 whole days. When he prayed God confirmed the same to him.

I met Rev. Emmanuel Twagirimana some couple of years after his resurrection.
When he spoke at my church the testimony as in other venues he'd been to, was received with a pinch of salt. Well, someone just had to establish the truth. I traveled to Rwanda to scout the facts – what came out in the villages, towns and at Kigali, was a word for word confirmation of the story Emmanuel told. I talked to a cross-section of church leaders who substantiated the death-and-back-to-life testimony.

I arranged for a breakfast get-together to provide Emmanuel with the platform to tell his story to many. The morning banquet, that ended up with people receiving Christ was attended by an assortment of government officials and church leaders, amongst many.

Seven Days in Heaven is not a story but a bona-fide compilation of events after death. The book talks candidly about the two places God has prepared for us to spend an eternity – depending on which is chosen. The book brings to life, **Luke 16:19-31** - where the story of the rich man and Lazarus is told. It is a reminder that there is an eternal destiny to live for today.

I recommend *Seven Days in Heaven* to you with the keenness a doctor recommends a medicinal dose – that carries a cure. Read it prayerfully and you will be blessed. The message in this book is life; I recommend it to you.

Bishop Dr A. Kitonga,
Apostolic Bishop of the Redeemed Gospel Church Inc.

INTRODUCTION

As a boy I heard stories of people dying and coming back to life; such fairy-tales, I would say and shrug off the high tales. But one day, I died and came back to life. That changed how I view life and what lies beyond it.

There is life after death. The Bible says that, after death follows judgment. Popular teachings would want to convince the world otherwise. Haven't we seen an influx of books, magazines and movies determined to portray Jesus Christ as a hoax messiah with nothing to offer to the world. Well, my point is this; such lies will forever be invented.

And, are we not living on the fast lane with businesses spilling over into new territories by the day; And by the day, institutions are graduating students whom, I only hope will find work after grueling schedules in class; New relationships are being initiated as old ones forge on or crumble. Newborns are making their entrance into the world with the first debut shriek only peculiar to babies. And yet, even though life is unfolding as usual you must never forget that – that will not always happen.

One day, very soon Christ will be returning. He is returning to punish sin and to reward righteousness. That's why, you must at every opportunity shun lies, and hold on to the truth. The truth is made plain in the Bible which is the inspired word of God.

And so, although somewhere, everywhere something important is happening, we must still give regard to tomorrow. The Bible provides evidence that, tomorrow, we will be rewarded either in heaven or in hell, for what we do or do not do today.

Once upon a time, a rich man who enjoyed a luxurious content life with no regard for God, died. Next door to him, a poor man who lived with high regard for God also died. The rich man's soul went to be tormented in hell, but Lazarus was carried up to sit at Abraham's bosom.

From this, it is apparent that two places destined are for the soul after death - **HEAVEN AND HELL.** I wonder which side you'd fall on, were the Lord to demand for your soul today.

When I died for seven days, Jesus took me on a tour of heaven; and a tour of hell. *7 Days In Heaven* is a story of my spiritual experience, of what I saw in both places; I recommend heaven. I have tried as best as possible to share the facts as clearly as I can remember them. Choose life. Choose heaven.

TABLE OF CONTENTS

Acknowledgements
Dedication
Foreward
Introduction

CHAPTER ONE 17
   BACKGROUND ON THE WAR 17
   THE PROPHECY 19
   BUSINESS 23
   LUKEWARM 24
   THE PRESIDENT IS ASSASINATED
   (April 6th, 1994) 28

CHAPTER TWO 31
   THE WAR BEGINS 31
   RESTLESS 33
   THE BOMB 35
   NO AMPUTATION 37
   NOWHERE TO RUN 41

CHAPTER THREE 47
   SPIRITUAL TOURS 47
   HEAVEN 47
   ANGELIC CHOIR 49
   MY CORPSE 50
   MANSIONS UP ABOVE 52
   THE OFFICE 54
   SAINTS 56

THE LETTER 60
THE GARDEN... 64
THE TABLE 66
WHITE STONE.. 68
THE TREE OF LIFE 68
HUMAN BODY PARTS 69
CROWNS... 70
HELL.. 71
SATAN'S AGENTS... 74

CHAPTER FOUR... 79
THE RESURRECTION 79
THE WAR IS OVER... 81

CHAPTER FIVE 85
DIVINE PROVISION.. 85

CHAPTER SIX... 93
HOME SWEET HOME 93
UMWANA W'UMWAMI
(CHILD OF THE KING) 97
THE DIVINE OPERATION.............................. 100
A NEW PREACHER... 103

CHAPTER SEVEN 105
TIME TO INVEST.. 105
RWANDA... 106
DEMOCRATIC REPUBLIC OF CONGO 107
TANZANIA.. 109
MWANZA, TANZANIA................................... 110
SOUTH AFRICA.. 116

BOMBAY- INDIA 116
OXFORD-ENGLAND 116
AIRBORNE, EGYPT AIR 117
ITALY 119
HEALING 119

CHAPTER EIGHT 123
WEDDING BELLS 123
FORGIVENESS 131
PLEASE STAND UP 134

Author Information 137

CHAPTER ONE

BACKGROUND ON THE WAR

In the dawn of a new decade a strange wind swept across my motherland; the year was 1990. The reformative waves blew across, touching and affecting the politically minded in ways we didn't understand until years later - precisely, four years later.

Among the politically inclined began a disturbing restlessness, a suppressed mood. The tension was almost tangible. Tangibility was made vivid by the reports we gathered from various sources. We picked this and that up from the dailies, the radio and over the grapevine. Listening, watching, reading and hearing were our portion, the lot of us anxious citizens unsure of what to expect when and if the tide subsided.

Obviously my mother country was in a transition, a force often claimed to be the catalyst pushing for better governance; whatever it was, it persisted unabated. I as everyone else watched obediently unable to predict the outcome. That was the birth of the clamor for multi-party politics.

In spite of the unfolding political display life went on. People everywhere carried on with work as usual. Some such as I, carried on with our affairs in the city. We kept business meetings with important clients, always in time for the next appointment. We worked hard in our offices, answering telephone calls; responding to letters, faxes like the rest of the world on their modern devices.

In the smaller towns, life was interactive. Middlemen suppliers and buyers haggled over prices. Children listened in classrooms; teachers taught disciplining mischief. Over in the country side, the fields and farms grew our food - the fruit and grain the cities and towns ate. Everyone everywhere fended for their livelihood.

Come 1991, it was obvious the tide was mounting not subsiding. Wrangles were evident within the government. Still we worked side by side Hutu and Tutsi for these are Rwanda's main ethnic groups. Oblivious of any differences we transacted and exchanged our wares. We loved one another freely, marrying each others sons and daughters. No one really cared what the other looked like, or came from.

I can't tell the exact point the rift between us began to show. Somehow we had known it existed but remained mum.

Almost suddenly, members belonging to either of the two tribes, Hutu and Tutsi, those from the North or South seemed conscious of their differences, economical, social or whatever.

THE PROPHECY

"Therefore thus says the Lord, If you return then I will bring you back; you shall stand before Me. If you take out the precious from the vile, you shall be as My mouth: let them return to you but you must

not return to them. And I will make you to these
people a fortified bronze wall; and they will fight
against you but they shall not prevail against you.
For I am with you to save you and deliver you,"
says the Lord.
I will deliver you out of the hand of the wicked and
I will redeem you from the grip of the Terrible,"
Jeremiah 15:19-21.

For very good reasons, this is one of my favourite Scriptures. I fall back on these words for comfort and illumination every so often. The reason I treasure them so much is because they came to me prophetically in the early stages of my quest for God, through a sister by the name Mariam, during a trip down to the Democratic Republic of Congo where I had gone to put a couple of things into effect. The fated meeting strengthens my confidence in divine connections. Certainly, God used Mariam to catapult me to the next level of my salvation.

At Kabela, a small village in an area called South Kivu, Mariam was popular as one could ever get. Her many visitors headed off literally skipping with contentment. People testified of having experienced the touch of God in a tangible way. Mainly, the source of the joy that was written all over the faces that left the premises was the brush with the manifest presence of God ever so present at Mariam's home.

The precision, with which her prophetic utterances came to pass, was famed from corner to corner. I considered myself lucky to be among those whom Mariam would see that day, back in 1989. Again, why I consider the meeting such an honour is because deep within I buried a strong desire to be used by God, in my generation. Coming face to face with Mariam only reinforced that desire.

I remember feeling Mariam's keen gaze on me. I couldn't tell what was going through her mind, but whatever it was it had to be some deep stuff. It did eventually spill out, in the prophetess' natural cool demeanor: **"God is going to use you as a witness to many nations and to different people. You will prophecy to leaders and kings. However, you will pass**

through difficult and painful times." The timely declaration confirmed a strong gut feeling; God was up to something major.

Soon after, Mariam announced that we needed to pray. She began slowly, almost inaudibly. Only gradually did the prayer pick tempo, as earnest intercession poured from her lips. A sudden flood of liberation streamed in sweeping relief throughout my entire being. Everything about life felt lighter, so much bearable. It's clear in my mind that, that day marked a turning point in my life. God lifted off a significant amount of the weight that easily beset me.

The brief prayer session packed me with renewed confidence, and faith – the kind that stops at nothing. I decided then, that no devil stood a chance against me. And so, with that zeal, my homeward journey commenced; it's mission clear – to seek God like never before; I was going to accomplish my purpose on earth.

BUSINESS

Back from that trip, Rwanda's tranquil years saw my rise and rise as a business force. By all means, God's grace kept me at the pinnacle of events. As I think over it now, it amazes me how every one of my ventures was big booming business. At the Coca-Cola depot, the soft drink sold in large quantities bringing in sums of money every year. Good success reflected in my clothing line. The grain store too was prosperous.

In all, good success reflected all around. That filled me with gladness. I refer to it as gladness because that's what I saw it to be. It never occurred to me that the satisfaction I enjoyed edged on pride or disobedience. Nothing along those lines pricked my conscience. 'No, that's not possible', I would comfort myself. I was blinded by the comfort that I still observed spiritual obligations — well at least some of them.

LUKEWARM

I'm unable to tell the exact point in time that my heart turned lukewarm towards Godly issues. I don't suspect that business success prompted the change of heart; I know for sure it was the cause of the reluctant state. Once in an instance of open defiance way back in 1993, I blatantly slighted an assignment to take a warning message to the President.

I had had a vision about my country. I saw in the vision the President dying, many Rwandan people killed, bodies in bushes and on streets, others floating on rivers. I saw water turning into blood, massive graves being dug.

God told me to go and tell the Head of the State to stop all the political meetings on Sundays and call people for repentance. Because people had left God, instead of going to worship on Sundays, they went to attend political meetings

God wanted the president to unite the Rwandan people more and to let those who lived in exile to come back to their land.

I did not go because of fear. Prayerlessness causes fear. Again, later in the year, the Holy Spirit directed me to go up to the Mount Kigali to preach; I never went.

Previously, especially soon after returning from the Democratic Republic of Congo, such decrees would not meet resistance. My earlier devotion was unquestionable. Commitment was sure notwithstanding time or distance.

Praying and fasting for a straight twenty-one or forty days was the custom, not a struggle.

It was in that spirit that I had formed a ministry. Spurred on by determination and the passionate to please God, the ministry began to grow by the double. Soon, there was a management team in place; and what resourceful people they were. God sent me the best. Together, we set out to make a difference in our community. It was unanimously agreed that the most effective was through an outreach ministry.

And so, we started an outreach division that oversaw; evangelistic campaigns, hospital missions and other outdoor tasks. The hospital visits were special to me because they provided a chance to care for the sick in hospital wards and other sick rooms. In all, we did the best we could to feed, clothe the sick; a chance to generally shower them with Christ's love. Most of the ones who recovered opted to join us.

Friday was my giving day. Come the fifth day of the week I would be ready to give. Time and resources were generously availed to meet and satisfy the needs of many families and homes who depended upon our generosity.

The tradition was so deeply ingrained that my accounts office knew to forward the day's profits to the cause without a reminder. For months, the system worked perfectly.

'Which sound thinking business person wastes away the most profitable day in the name of love?' After so many Giving Friday's, I began to find the tradition damn ridiculous. I questioned my generous hand, finding the whole thing silly all over a sudden. Suddenly it was an unwise business move; after all, we recorded voluminous sales every Friday. I questioned the intelligence of our generosity settling that any other day would be as ideal but, certainly not Friday.

Though that decision was settled on earth, heaven felt otherwise about the new me. The Holy Spirit began convicting me so relentlessly causing total lack of peace. Although I knew God was trying to get me to understand some things, I totally ignored Him. I remember receiving this particular message so many times, "God wants you in fulltime ministry."

The message was delivered by different people at different times. It was obvious He saw the complacency brought on by my business accomplishment, and He was demanding for my full attention. He saw the stumbling block called success. God sent warning messages saying He would wipe out all my entire fortune, if I didn't return to Him.

'I don't see how that is possible,' I would reason to myself. My obvious influence in Rwanda's markets was felt. I was rich and successful. 'I can make it and I'm making it,' I concluded and never changed, never obeyed. Falling back more each day, my spiritual life deteriorated. Prayer became a struggle. Once a forty-day fasting prayer champion, now even three days of fasting was a real hurdle.

THE PRESIDENT IS ASSASINATED
(April 6th, 1994)

The music in my house played softly soothing off the strain after a tedious day. Sitting back, I soaked in the enjoyable play needing no company or disturbance. Abruptly, rather impolitely, the tune on air was cut off and replaced with a stern order. "Nobody should leave their house!" Everyone was advised to remain indoors. As abruptly as the radio message, so was the change of scene outdoors. No longer was it safe or possible to linger out in the streets.

Previously all the hustle Rwanda knew was the hum of motor vehicle engines and the bargaining pleas of buyers and sellers. In a split second terror ruled and walked where we walked and transacted safely. Overnight Kigali, and other towns and centers were no go battle-zones. Gun shots, explosions, fires and random attacks took centre stage. The atmosphere was tense promising evil.

The war which exploded in its ruthlessness to become among the worst to ever be witnessed began as talk in the radio. Whether real or assumed, speculations on the war unleashed tension that stole the joy from of our daily routines. Though nothing was official we could tell that all was not well within the government. Fears were confirmed gradually, painfully. That's when homes, schools, shops and our favourite meeting spots began to be deserted.

The fields were abandoned.

CHAPTER TWO

THE WAR BEGINS

The war forced me back to submission. I have since learnt never to harden my heart, to degrees where God's hand of chastisement must force me into submission. God wants to draw us to Himself through His love, and never through chastisement.

Four of us met in my house to pray for our nation, far gone in an internal power struggle. Our little prayer group was comprised of an employee, my sister and Simon, a man who'd traveled all the way from countryside to seek shelter in my house. Simon was extremely prayerful.

We prayed intensely. With gunshots, slayings, rape and other forms of brutality going on, we were desperate for God. Our teary prayers were pleas, and more pleas for His protection;

that God would stop the bombs, arson and break-ins.

God is faithful. His Word came to us, ***"Do not be afraid. I will protect you."*** This encouraged us so much, that we stepped up the intercession.

One day the sound of heavy banging on our door interrupted our prayers. We were shaken, expecting the worst. The banging persisted. The opened door, of course after a moment of hesitation, revealed the figure of a pregnant woman.

The tearful woman, trembled with fear and anxiety, coupled with a mixture of other pained emotions. Only the most heartless would close their back to such open desperation. I recognized her as one who'd regularly bought supplies from my shop.

Moved by her condition, we let her in. She explained that her people had forced her out of a house, or shelter they were staying. Whatever the story, she was now with us. Life had to continue, somehow. The woman was tired. She winced in distress, the most I could do was to assure her of God's protection. She settled in; now one of us.

Two days later, the woman's distress mounted. Apparently she was due to deliver. I was disturbed about it, and clearly, so was everyone else. Why had God send a pregnant woman our way anyway; I questioned, but He didn't answer. Anyway, not so long afterwards, the cry of pain that ushers newborns into the world filled the house. Later, much later, two little babies made their entrance into the world.

RESTLESS

2nd May found me extremely disturbed. I was more restless than ever since the war's outbreak. I had the most uneasy knowing feeling within that something unusual lay ahead. For some reason I sensed impending harm.

Driven by my restlessness, I ventured out to a neighboring house where brethren had gathered for prayers. Little did I know that I walked into the place where I would get a confirmation to the messages I'd heard so many times before: "You will go through very tough times." The bearer of the prophecy further confirmed that it was time for the fulfillment of every prophecy I had ever received.

Later, the man who'd delivered the message invited me over to his house for further prayers. I was reluctant to go. Though I politely turned down the request, he would hear none of it and so, I followed him to his home. Sticking to his intent for inviting me over, we began to pray.

Suddenly, I saw the most ghastly sight. It was a bloody, ugly and cruel scene. I forced my eyes open, shaking, so terribly afraid of what I'd seen in the vision. I narrated the incident to my prayer partner who shocked me when he said that he'd seen a similar vision; detail by detail. In that state, I rose to say goodbye longing to get away. I just needed the familiarity of my home.

My host would hear of no excuse. He firmly insisted that I stay over for a supper of boiled potatoes, and some stew. I just wanted to leave. Attempting to make an exit once more I said that I had no desire to eat. Studying me intently my host said that God had prepared a place for me to go. He said it was best we carry on praying, after supper.

THE BOMB

What came next happened too fast. I'm unable to tell clearly what exactly took place. I remember a rough lifting motion. The next thing I know is being thrown to the ground violently. Pain, extreme pain overpowered me, it split through my entire body. I also recall the man shouting 'He's dying, he's dying.' People came to find out what had happened, they found me in extreme pain. I remember being put into a car.

Next, I found myself lying on a simple bed inside a crowded room - a hospital room it soon became apparent. I find it difficult to express the state of the ward at *Centre Hospitalier De Kigali.* Blood, bandages, tears, were all that one was able to see. Groans of anguish were let out continuously, from every corner of the room.

The fate awaiting me was revealed by a doctor doing rounds, "We have to amputate your hand and leg," he said pointing at my incapacitated limbs. My left hand was a mess. It was literally shredded to bits by the bomb that had hit the house on that tragic day. My left leg too had suffered grave injuries. Scrutinizing me the doctors' face seemed to warm as he registered recognition. I believe he recognized me from the hospital missions back then. "We will not amputate you," he said, as an after thought. "You cared for the sick," he went on as, as he walked out.

People died by the minute as I watched. The fear of death struck me with terror. For dear life I clung to **Psalms Chapter 91**. *"He who* *dwells in the secret place of the Most High shall abide under the shadow of the Almighty.*

I will say of the Lord, "He is my refuge and my fortress: my God; in Him will I trust."

Surely, He shall deliver you from the snare of the fowler and from the perilous pestilence. He shall cover you with His feathers, and under His wings you shall take refuge: His truth shall be thy shield and buckler.

You shall not be afraid for the terror by night; nor for the arrow that flies by day; nor for pestilence that walks in darkness; nor the destruction that lays waste at noonday.

A thousand shall fall at your side, and ten thousand at your right hand; but it shall not come nigh you."

"I will not die; God said I'm not going to die," I prayed out aloud.

NO AMPUTATION

"It's impossible to stitch these back," the man said with a sneer. The words reached me on the operating table where I was stretched out for examination. The doctor, a different one, expressed his inability to save my limbs, as he looked for the first time at the full extent of the damage done. "These have to be amputated immediately," he continued on the same vein, with a stern finger pointing at the gone limbs.

In as much as I was in pain, I argued that I wasn't ever going to be amputated on - come rain, come shine, come whatever! Taken back by my stubbornness, the doctor hastily redid the bandages, without any regard of the agony his rough handling put me through and, threw me out in the corridor to await fates decision.

The torture was extreme such as I cannot explain. After what seemed like an eternity, the doctor who'd recognized me earlier, walked by. As he helped me on to a bed, I dared not mention that I had not received proper treatment. Just then, an explosion rocked the entire hospital. "What was that; what happened?' It was no need asking; no need expecting an answer. We all knew what had happened; a bomb had hit the hospital.

Mostly, those who died from that particular explosion were the ones lying along the corridor. I didn't even want to think about it, considering I had been out there in the corridor just minutes earlier. My doctor friend commented saying, "surely you won't die because most of the people in the corridor where I moved you from have just died from the bomb!"

After several days of lying in bed untreated I began to experience a peculiar sensation in my wounds; more like a movement. I couldn't tell exactly what was going on because the slightest touch on the bandaged parts brought extreme pain. The movements, small and irritating continued confirming the worst – there were maggots in my wounds.

All day long, all week long the explosions continued. A house of torment is the most fitting description of the hospital after a series of bomb raids. What was once a decent sickbay was turned into a ruin, a nightmare for those of us unfortunate to be there. Those able to walk fled to safer zones of their own accord as patients were advised to move to either of two other provincial hospitals.

I knew I had to leave at some point, the only question was - who would ferry me elsewhere? It was a question I had begun to worry about.

One morning a man came to pick up a patient, either a friend or relative I'm not sure which, but I'm glad that the person he'd come for had found alternative means of transport.

He accepted to give me a ride. The painful trip to a different hospital was in vain. Hospitals overflowed with patients, forcing overseers to turn new patients away. Most, such as we were re-directed to school compounds and classrooms serving as makeshift hospitals and clinics for treatment.

From a distance one could tell that space in the school compound was fully occupied. Queues of white bandages lingering everywhere, met our eyes. No room was available, all was occupied save for the tiny space I was squeezed into.

Apparently the make-shift hospital was the extension of a Catholic hospital. Nuns attended to the many casualties, waiting their turn. I knew the moment I dreaded the most, when bandages would have to be undone was coming. It did inevitably - hands maneuvered, attempting to unwind the pieces of cloth.

The pain caused me to yell out. It was extreme more than I could bear and so someone opted to pour in a medicinal fluid through the dirty bandages, for there was no undoing them. Of course, the injuries on my leg and hand deserved more expert treatment. But such expertise was no where to be found and anyway, the pain was excruciating.

NOWHERE TO RUN

Our safety was temporal. Sounds of gunfire neared our compound. The approaching militia men destabilized the calm. The fighting had caught up with me, again. Nuns, our source of hope, fled for their safety. Those who were able to move fled too. Sleep and rest, for those of us left behind, weak and incapacitated came in disturbed bouts. We were a bunch of panic-stricken folk, always anticipating the worst.

One day, a group of armed men stormed into our classroom. Oh, they breathed malice. "No need wasting any bullets, kill them with the swords," one rough voice in the mob suggested. The bloodthirsty remark was followed by screams from the panicky patients. It was chaotic. Amid the chaos a still small voice whispered to me, *"it's the devil using them to do all this!' Tell them to forgive the killers!*

In bold obedience I raised my voice and shouted; "Forgive them." For a moment all was still. Stern faces focused on me. "Are you saved?" someone asked. The man lying next to me readily answered "yes!" The militia men appeared softened by the response. Oblivious to them the ready answer was given by Haji Idrissa, a devout Muslim until that moment when he said yes.

"We can't kill these people," I heard one of the men say. To our surprise they backed off leaving us overjoyed.

Haji Idriss got saved there.

The peace left behind was received by starving patients so tormented by physical anguish. We were a bunch of paining people, hungry as wolves; left behind to attend to our wounds and to fend for our stomachs.

Anything that could find its way to the mouth was devoured. Pangs of hunger were cutting through my stomach and maggots were biting me like thousands of syringes.

Overcome by hunger, I watched agape as some people peeled off and ate their own flesh. Others would crawl about and feel in the garbage for bits of rotten foodstuff thrown in the litter, God knows when. Sad to say, but whatever they could garner was usually contaminated by human flesh.

Due to my state, open wounds and all, I couldn't crawl around for food. Also, I wasn't able to solicit for bits of whatever rots was being consumed, for I was too weak to speak. And so, I lay on the floor waiting for either sickness or hunger, or both to take me out, - for sure, one was bound to take us all out - one by one.

Strange and I can't tell why, but at some point my hunger vanished completely. I stopped being bothered at all starvation. My vision was however, severely affected. I couldn't focus straight or clearly and saw double vision. The classroom seemed to rotate at a high speed and I closed my eyes because it was disturbing.

I began to feel as if I was ascending, more as though my body was being lifted up in slow motion. It was the first joyous feeling I'd felt in ages. I gave in to the slow heady feeling not understanding what it was or where it was leading.

Suddenly, the feeling faded giving way to the awakening realization that I was standing in front of a massive entrance. Once more, clear vision had returned. I gawked around in wonder marveling at everything, including the attire I suddenly found myself in. It was a beautiful flowing white gown.

I noticed then, that I wasn't alone. Someone stood in front of me. I never saw him come, for he was instantly there, beaming sweetly.

Besides being engagingly cheerful, the man was very handsome. *"I am an angel,"* he introduced himself. I suddenly realized his wings.

"You are standing at heaven's gateway," he continued beautifully. All I could do was staring, dumbfounded. *"Jesus has directed me to take you where He is,"* the angel went on as he strode forward. I took this as the cue to follow him. The motion prompted the gate to open up of its own accord. Behind us the doors closed obediently. My angel companion and I walked through side by side, in silent companionship.

CHAPTER THREE

SPIRITUAL TOURS

HEAVEN

I believe that a description of heaven's magnificence is not humanly possible. I know that I walked on gold, streets made of gold but, fall short in describing things with the precision they deserve. Sweet flowers in all beautiful colours line the gold paved streets. The flowers let out a glorious smell, a divine scent that fills the atmosphere beautifully. The flowers adhere to a musical rhythm, a worship tune of their own, for they opened and closed in unison, releasing a rainbow of colours, at intervals, as we walked by.

I'm not too sure at what point my feet were lifted off the ground, for at some point, although we walked, our feet never touched the ground. Our pace was also incredibly accelerated. In that rate and fashion, I was

47

presented before an awesome throne. Somehow, without asking I knew who sat there; I knew that it was Jesus Christ occupying His throne in true Kingly splendour. I observed Him in awe, taking in His breathtaking presence in wonder.

Jesus spoke for the first time since my entry. It was a welcoming greeting. His hands were soft and warm; the sound of His voice filled me with merry causing me to break out in laughter. The laughter was uncontrollable, the kind you can't stop and don't care to stop. I laughed and laughed some more as Jesus watched me.

"I am Jesus Christ. I was dead but now I am live. Whoever believes in me finds eternal life," Jesus said. He suddenly took on His earthly form. He showed me the marks on His hands and feet, scars that evidenced His crucifixion on the cross. In a brief while, He was back in His glorified form. *"I've brought you to heaven to show you the reward for those who serve the Lord."* Jesus explained that His, is the seat of Mercy and He forgives everyone who

48

calls on His name for forgiveness. *"Without salvation no one shall enter heaven,"* He made it plain and with that we began to stroll.

ANGELIC CHOIR

Jesus went on to show me the great angelic choir. They cut the image of true royalty with celestial bodies and golden teeth, in sparkling white flowing gowns. I noticed that they had all manner of instruments such as I have never seen all of a beautiful shimmering gold; golden guitars, golden trumpets and so on. As they flapped their wings in unison, a beautiful melody as the sound of a series of drums being played, was produced. In that precise moment, I could sing along, word for word. Jesus turned to me with a knowing smile and said, *"When you return to earth you won't remember any of these songs."*

"These," He illumined pointing in the choir's direction *"sing and celebrate whenever someone on earth receives Me."* Jesus explained that the angelic choir applause is the

first reward, sinners receive on accepting salvation. Angels celebrate jubilantly when as much as one sinner turns to God. The heavenly choir mesmerized me totally. I observed and listened to them in deep appreciation. Were, it left to me; I would have stood there forever. Knowing this Jesus said, *"I want to show you other sights."* We proceeded.

MY CORPSE

"I want to show you your corpse back on earth." In a flash second, Jesus and I, were suspended in mid-air watching the proceedings in the room. My remains lying at the back of the classroom in the makeshift hospital came into view. Quite oblivious of our presence, the sick and forlorn patients moped about in hopelessness. Some appeared to be crying over my death. I smiled thinking to myself, 'You should be crying for your souls.' I suddenly had a really strong impulse to touch them but Jesus stopped me.

My decomposing remains were wrapped in beddings, secured by ropes; that had once bound sticks of firewood, that were heaped in one corner of the room. Jesus fixed me a studying gaze and asked *"Now you've seen. What can you compare yourself to?"* I looked back at the dead body unable to offer an ideal response. "I am like a rotting cow," I said softly. *"That's not a cow; it's your earthly body. You are not recognizing your earthly body because you are now in this heavenly body.*

Many people value what they see, but do not care for eternal things. But if the glamour of the heavenly body would be revealed to them, they would give up everything to inherit it.

1 Corinthians Chapter 15, leads us to believe that indeed, *There are also celestial bodies and terrestrial bodies but the glory of the celestial is one, and the glory of the terrestrial is another.* **1 Corinthians 15:40.**

It is good, even important to hit the gym, and other health spas, having health practices and going to health clubs but, as much as we care

51

for the outer part we should care for the inner man who shall see the Kingdom of God.

Life is all about striking healthy balances. Grooming the outer man may help us to live longer but - grooming the inside man will help us to live forever. Our hearts need to be cleaned regularly through the reading of the Word and prayers.

MANSIONS UP ABOVE

In My Father's house are many mansions; if it were not so, I would have told you. I go to prepare a place for you. And if I go and prepare a place for you, I will come again and receive you to Myself: that where I am, there you may be also," **John 14: 2-3**.

Jesus read the Scripture from a scroll. We had just ascended for an extended tour of heaven, and were walking down a street that was lined with inordinate mansions. The homes were extremely beautiful, so creatively constructed. **"These** *are the mansions I have said are in my Father's House,"* He said pointing ahead. *"You* *shall witness about them when you go back to earth."*

I observed though, that some mansions were more striking than others. Some were incomplete ending at the window level. Surprised, I inquired about the differences. *"The beautiful ones"* Jesus said, **"belong to the believers who walk in holiness and serve Me faithfully with all their hearts. Their works and offerings proceed to heaven to beautify their mansions."**

"What of the others?" I asked pointing at the incomplete homes. *"The owners were faithful but they slackened and so their mansions stalled,"* Jesus replied. *"The ones bellow window levels are for those who no longer serve Me"* It hit me that He was referring to backsliders. *"I am sending My servants to wake them up so that they will serve Me as they used to. If they are disobedient God will give away the mansions for others to complete. I am coming soon to take away My church. I will not come for those whose mansions are incomplete."*

Jesus folded the scroll somehow converting it into a piece of bread. *"Open your mouth,"* He instructed. I obeyed. The bread was gently placed in my mouth. It was sweet tasting like honey. *"I have placed a Bible in your heart. You will understand all the languages so as to speak to all people, whenever you do not have an interpreter, I will fill you with the Holy Spirit and you will speak in their language Don't stop. Go to all nations,"* Jesus instructed me saying, *"You must continue reading the printed Word for the sake of the people."*

THE OFFICE

We walked into what appeared to be an office block. Jesus confirmed this saying the building housed the angel's offices. A large volume lay on one of the tables. I stared at the book, curious to know its contents. *"It's the Book of Life,"* Jesus answered my curious mind, as His fingers played with the pages which I noticed had two distinct columns. One side listed names and, next to the name in a different column, were detailed explanations of the person's actions.

In short, all our doings, good or bad are recorded in the Book of Life. The works recorded is what God will use to judge us. *"And I saw the dead, small and great, stand before God, and the books were opened. And another book was opened, which is the book of life. And the dead were judged according to their works, by the things which were written in the books."* **Rev 20:12.**

I was amazed at the whole system; Jesus took opportunity to elaborate the benefits of serving God. He referred me where Tabitha was brought back to life because of her good deeds.

Then Peter arose and went with them. When he had come, they brought him into the upper room. And all the widows stood by him weeping, and showing the tunics and garments which Dorcas made while she was with them. But Peter put them all out and knelt down and prayed. And turning him to the body said, "Tabitha, arise ". And she opened her eyes, and when she saw Peter, she sat up. Then he gave her his hand and lifted herup; and when he had called the saints and the widows, presented her alive." **Acts 9: 39-41.**

SAINTS

I was still thinking of the benefits of serving God as we left the office block and proceeded to *"the place the righteous go after death."* There was a massive, deep and terrifying sea. Jesus pointed beyond it saying, *"The righteous live across."*

A great multitude kept coming to Jesus. He received them warmly. Jesus quelled my open-mouthed gaze with the reassuring voice I had come to love so much, *"They have finished their work and have come from different parts of the world. There are some from your country, Rwanda,"* He said. *"I am taking them to their rest. Then I heard a voice from heaven saying to me, write: blessed are the dead who die in the Lord from now on: Yes, says the spirit, "that they may rest from their labors; and their works follow them."* **Rev 14:13.**

"I am the way, the truth and the life. No one comes to the Father except through Me," Jesus quoted from John 14:6. No one but I is able to take people to the home of the righteous.

The home of the righteous is in actual fact an assembly of people who died right with God. Remember, when I died I took on spiritual body and when a person is in heaven he has the spirit of revelation. So I was able to recognize other saints including some like Enoch, Stephen, Mary, Paul... - who lived on before me. I tried to speak to them but my voice couldn't reach to their side. Jesus gave me something like a pair of binoculars, and looking through it, I was able to talk clearly. Their joy was contagious and I wanted to join them, but Jesus stopped me, for anyone who reaches that place never comes back. *"I want you to go back to earth and tell people what you have seen."*

I suddenly noticed the obvious absence of two significant people I had worked with in the ministry. They had passed on and gone to heaven, or so we thought. "Where are they?" I enquired. *"Their hearts remained in the world,"* Jesus said referring to our ministry's caterer, and treasurer. *"The treasurer came out of the world but the world never came out of him, he was not honest with funds. He lied about the ministry's finances claiming that money was stolen when in actual fact He had spent it."* I remembered the instances. "But he loved you!" I countered. *"Even Judas Iscariot though he was my disciple, he did not inherit the Kingdom of God"* Jesus answered me. "What about the caterer?"

"She got saved, but her heart remained in Sodom and Gomorrah," The woman Jesus talked of was in-charge of the food unit during our hospital missions. She had died after a short illness - extremely bitter and angry at everyone who never went to see her at the hospital, Jesus disclosed. He said that on her deathbed she vowed, never to forgive.

Prior to her death God had sent messages urging her to forgive and let go. She refused, adamantly hanging on the offence. She died in that state.

Jesus talked to me about forgiveness saying that He forgave His persecutors at the cross. He talked about Stephen who also forgave and released those who stoned him.

It suddenly struck me that Jesus Had never introduced me to His father and I asked, "You have not showed me the Father?" *"If you have seen Me you have seen the Father."* **John 14:9** was His reply.

Earlier I had seen far behind the home of the righteous, twenty four elders and four living creatures. The elders had a very glorious and heavenly beauty. I could not see them clearly but in their hands they had things which appeared like precious viols and they were worshipping but whom they worshiped I could not see clearly. *"Now when He had taken the scroll, the four living creatures and twenty four elders fell down before the Lamb, each having a harp, and golden bowls full of incense, which are the prayers of Saints"* **Revelation 5:8**

THE LETTER

The letter highlights reasons why spiritual people will not enter heaven. In brief it mentions that;

i.   To inherit eternal life one must be saved. The **unsaved:** those who do not receive Jesus Christ as their saviour will not enter heaven. Those whose names are no written in the book of life cannot enter in heaven. *"And anyone not found written in the book of life was cast in to the lake of fire"* **Revelation 20:15**

ii. To inherit eternal life, a believer must be forgiving; **unforgiveness** is in most cases the source of bitterness, jealousy, gossip, malice and strives.
"Pursue peace with all people, and holiness, without which no one will see The Lord; looking carefully lest anyone fall short of the grace of God, lest any root of bitterness springing up cause

trouble, and by this many become defiled. **Hebrews 12: 14-15.**

But if you do no forgive, neither will your father in Heaven forgive your trespasses" **Mark 11:26**

iii.   To inherit eternal life a believer must **tithe**. Non-payment of tithe amounts to robbing. Tithe is not meant for the poor, it is for the house of God. *"Will a man rob God? Yet you have robbed Me! But you say "In what way have we robbed you? "In tithes and offerings. You are cursed with a curse, for you have robbed Me, even this whole nation. Bring all the tithes into the storehouse, that there may be food in My house, and try Me now in this," says the Lord of hosts,* **Malachi 3: 8-10**

Church leaders and servants of God should tithe faithfully, even a tenth part of the tithes received from their congregations.

"Speak thus to the Levites, and say to them: when you take from the children of Israel the tithes which I have given you from them as

your inheritance, then you shall offer up a heave offering of it for the Lord, a tenth of the tithe" **Numbers 18: 26**

"To bring the first fruit of our dough, our offering, the fruit of all manner of trees, the new wine and oil, to the priest, to the storerooms of the house of our God; and to bring the tithes of our ground to the Levites , for the Levites should receive the tithes in all our farming communities. And the priest, the descendent of Aaron, shall bring up a tenth of the tithes to the house of our God, to the rooms of the storehouse **Nehemiah 10: 37-38.**

Jesus explained that in some instances the problems and poverty people suffer are entirely of their own making.

He spoke about Ananias and Sapphira, saying that Sapphira's greatest mistake was getting used to the servant of God Peter. She exemplifies the kind of foolishness referred to us in **Proverbs 27:22** *"Though you grind a fool in* *a mortar with a pestle along with crushed grain, yet his foolishness will not depart from him*

It is important to give more than just our tithe, but also other offerings. *"Honour The Lord with your possessions, and with the first fruits of all your increase; so your barns will be filled with plenty, and your vats will overflow with new wine"* **Proverbs 3:9-10.**

iv.   To inherit eternal life a believer must keep, fulfill his/her **VOWS.** Many believers never bother to honour their vows.   However He spoke about Jephtat, a man who diligently honoured his vow. The story found in **Judges 11:30-40**

> *"When you make a vow to God, do not delay to pay it; for He has no pleasure in fools. Pay what you have vowed, better not to vow than to vow and not pay. Do not let your mouth cause your flesh to sin, nor say before the messenger of God that it was an error. Why should God be angry at your excuse and destroy the work of your hands?* **Ecclesiastes 5: 4-6.**

Vows open up blessings. **Genesis 28: 20-22.**

As you are about to see- Satan never fights fair. As his name, fallen angel suggests, he is sneaky, crafty forever scheming your next fall. That's why you must forever be vigilant; sealing all gateways he may want to use to assert his authority. For one, he does assign some demons to keep people from giving to God. Satan knows that if we give, not only are we blessed, but the gospel is advanced. The solution however, is not shying away from making vows especially if we are in a position to fulfill them. If we shy away, we deny ourselves the chance to receive from God.

THE GARDEN

Severally in this book, I have been unable to describe what I saw down to the last detail, or with the exact precision that some scenes deserve. The garden scene is one of those. I was awed when Jesus took me there to marvel at what I believe is reverential beauty.

We stood in a picturesque garden, serene yet alive with splendorous plant life. There were graceful flowers and trees in full bloom, some laden with attractive fruit perfectly manicured lawns skirted the landscape, as far as the eye could possibly see. The mystical garden was awake, blooming with sweet scents. The trees swayed gently, most gracefully as if bowing, at the entrance of the Saviour. *"These different types of grapes will be used to make drinks and other fruits for the fruit salad, at feast when the Saints shall eat together with Me"* Jesus told me.

At the garden, the saints will greet, embrace each other. They will know each other;

On the other side, there was the sea of glass. It was beautiful beyond imagination, the sight left me speechless. *"Here the saints will have great joy. You will speak one language, and you will all have celestial bodies"* Jesus said.

"And I saw something like a sea of glass mingled with fire, and those who have the victory over the number of his name, standing on the sea of glass,

having the harps of God. They sing the song of the Lamb, saying: Great and marvelous are Your works, Lord God Almighty! Just and true are your ways, O King of saints. **Revelation 15:2-3**

Jesus said pointing at the beauty ahead.

THE TABLE

I followed Him to a big table the spot, He said, the saints will one day gather for to feast in kingly fashion. The meal is recorded in the book of Luke. *"But you are those who have continued with Me in My trials. And I bestow upon you the kingdom, just as My Father bestowed one upon Me. That you may eat and drink at My table in My Kingdom, and sit on thrones judging the twelve tribes of Israel,"* **Luke 22: 28-30.**

The table stood elegantly, neatly laid with cutlery. The chairs are extremely beautiful,(I have been privileged to visit homes of some prominent people but I have never sat in a chair as beautiful as the one I saw in Heaven)

With one hand outstretched towards the dining table, Jesus described the manner in which the saints, will sit to eat and drink with Him, forgetting earthly troubles. At that point it seemed important to ask Him if He was ever aware of my day to day earthly troubles. *"Yes, I was always aware of everything; that's why I sent My servants with a word of encouragement."* He said. I did not taste the food, I just looked at it and admired that the angels were good cooks.

The angels are eager to see *Jesus' bride.*

WHITE STONE

We walked on to a place lined with many white stones. Inscribed on every stone was a name which Jesus said, would be revealed to the person to receive the stone, on His return *"And I will give him a white stone, and on the stone a new name written which no one knows except him who receives it."* **Revelation 2:17.** Jesus said the weight of the stones varies depending on the saints output on earth.

"Tell them to work hard to better their reward for I am coming back soon for them." Jesus said as He steered me in the direction of the Tree of Life.

THE TREE OF LIFE

I observed how beautiful were the tree of life and its fruits, and Jesus told me that those who have been cleansed, and their robes are washed white will eat from the Tree of Life. *"And behold, I am coming quickly, and my reward is with*

Me, to give to everyone according to his work. I am the Alpha and the Omega, the Beginning and the End, the First and the last. Blessed are those who do My commandments that they may have the right to the tree of life, and may enter through the gates into the city," **Rev 22 12-14.**

HUMAN BODY PARTS

From there, Jesus led me to a magnificent storehouse. It was a very special experience for the house stores human body parts. There were eyes, hearts, kidneys, blood; every conceivable human part. Jesus explained that the stored parts replace ailing ones when a sick person on earth prays claiming healing. Angelic doctors perform a divine restorative surgery replacing the bad, worn out part with a brand new one picked from the storehouse. The person receives miraculous healing. Sometimes healing is instant. In some instances, change is not immediate but a gradual restoration whereby, wholeness is felt with time.

CROWNS

Next, we toured the place where saint's crowns - those for who lived long before us including those of our day are stored. Some crowns are big and others are small; some are simple while others are extravagant, all depending on ones' service to the Lord. One sweet day, the Lord will place a beautiful crown on your head, if you continue fighting the good fight of faith.

Jesus showed and explained to me many other things which I will share when the Lord releases me to do so.

HELL

"Now I will show you around hell," announced Jesus. In a while we stood in a dark surrounding. I hurdled closer to Jesus as I followed Him to the devil's quarters. Satan was stark naked, his skin was rough and he had a big wound on the forehead. I stared at the big wound.

Noting this Jesus said, *"It's not just my light that strikes him down. I have given the saints the Word HALLELUIAH to strike him down. When they say Halleluiah, Satan falls down. That is why the word is the same in every language. And that is why the wound on his head never dries."* Jesus went on to say that He created simultaneous seasons of darkness and light in the world so that He is continuously worshiped globally. That way the devil is constantly knocked down.

A slow fire burnt lazily, a few feet from where Satan fell. The slow flame promised to burn vengefully one day. On that day, Satan, his demons, followers, will be thrown into the lake, for it will be a lake of fire because of disobeying Christ. Satan knows this, that the fire is reserved for him in short while. *"Woe to the inhabitants of the earth and the sea! For the devil has come down to you, having great wrath, because he knows that he has a short time,"* **Rev: 12: 12b.**

The walk in hell opened my eyes to see and understand many things. I saw the people who died as sinners. They were working and tired. The lukewarm believers were on the other side, they are always bitten by demons.

Hell is horrid. It is a torture chamber more foul than our imaginations can know. Cries of pain from the souls trapped there, and from demons alike never cease. Hell is reserved for those who willfully reject God to entertain the flesh. *"But the cowardly, unbelieving, abominable, murderers, sexual immoral, sorcerers, idolaters, and all liars, shall have their part in the lake which burns with fire and brimstone, which is the second death".* **Rev 21:8.**

Those who do not pay their tithes faithfully, those who do not fulfill their vows are candidates of hell

Demons have been warned to "fear the genuine worshippers." When demons are rebuked authoritatively God's power strikes them paralyzing them completely. Some demons will break a host's limbs in the struggle to break free when God's power is released on them. Rescue demons rush for the injured ones in baskets to ferry them to 'safety.' These angry, injured demons go to unleash revenge on the people in hell (those who were lukewarm believers) through many violent acts like biting, scratching etc. And because they can't die such is the way those in hell are awaiting for judgment day.

Jesus then showed me the two members of our ministry, I had asked for during heaven's tour. We recognized each other. "You do not belong here," one exclaimed. "Go back and tell our people to be genuine Christians." I was being sent back to carry a warning message asking their families to live authentic Christian lives - to escape hell's torture.

Hell has factories that manufacture all manner of goods and products. Goods made there tally with exact precision with those made here on earth; talk of alcohol, cigarettes, clothes etc. Most especially, the consumables are packaged in sachets to make them easily accessible, and most of all affordable to recipients here.

SATAN'S AGENTS

At that point, Christ began warning me against Satan's agents, more so sorcerers and witch-doctors, who are in covenant relationship with Satan.

These perform 'miracles' to counterfeit the genuine works of Christ. They will do anything to convince you, they have all power - even if it means calling fire down from heaven. They use water and a black powder in their rituals.

Services are never for free, and large sums of money will be demanded in the pretense that lasting solutions will be offered.

Witchdoctors do convert themselves into different shapes and forms to access a given destination; or to perform a particular task. In whichever form they are; whether a bird, a stone or an animal - they still retain human understanding.

Cemeteries and especially large masses of water are the entry points for the mediums to and from hell.

God forbids the consultation from witches, mediums and other spiritual practices in which demons are depended upon. *Give no regard to mediums and familiar spirits; do not seek after them, to be defiled by them: I am the LORD your God."* **Leviticus 19:31**

There shall not be found among you any one who makes his son or his daughter pass through the fire, or one who practices witchcraft, or a soothsayer, or one who interprets omens, or a sorcerer... you shall be blameless before the LORD your God." **Deuteronomy 18:10, 13**

And please don't go for the next fashion blindly - certain fashion fads and trends are hell's brain child. They are formulated there and introduced here with the aim of luring people into sexual impurity. Satan wants to masquerade as good but he is evil and so are his deeds. It is his wish to fill the earth with indecency and immorality.

Largely, girls are used to pass on demonic trends and lifestyles. His bait is usually scantily dressed women, luring men to sin. And yes, sometimes demons do pose as humans, mostly beautiful women – depending on Satan's agenda.

The wares designed and manufactured in hell are produced purely to sheer enticement either to pull girls to prefer **lesbianism** or, men to love **homosexuality.** Demons do influence cultures causing men to basically carry on like women, by dressing like them — the road to homosexuality.

Piercing of unnatural body parts which is the trend today is a hellish culture. It is unfortunate that we ape things so ignorantly. Christians must be cautious about the fashions they adopt.

Satan assigns demons to distract church services. Satan will use every available tool and method to make sure people leave the church having grasped nothing.
Certain demons are sent to rouse an unnatural desire for food especially during praying and fasting. Sadly some demons sent succeed at instigating gossip, tribal and racial animosity among believers.

The information concluded hell's tour and shortly, we were back in heaven. *"I'm sending you back to earth,"* Jesus said kindly. I resisted but Christ talked to me about the importance of my journey back. He gave me the following Scriptures meant as an anchor in the return **(Colossians 2: 20; Hebrew 12: 14-17; Matthew 24: 14; Acts 26: 8; Romans 12: 17-21).**

"**Do *not fear*,**" Christ said firmly, "**Angels *are on guard*.**" Jesus promised to release angels to guide and guard me on the mission ahead. *"Go, I will be with you!"*

Those were Jesus parting Words. When I attempted to resist, He touched me lightly with His pointing finger - a sending away motion I perceived, indeed it was, and instantaneously I was back in my earthly form.

I left heaven with the sound warning that Satan would fight me hard for exposing him, but not before Jesus quoted Jeremiah Chapter one, *"Therefore prepare yourself and arise, and speak to them all that I command you. Do not be dismayed before their faces, lest I dismay you before them... they will fight against you, but they shall not prevail against you, for I am with you," says the Lord, "to deliver you,"* **Jeremiah 1:17, 19.**

It was a comforting reassurance - the knowledge that I wouldn't be alone. Whenever it's tough on the road I sense the presence of my guardian angels but it was not compared to staying there in heaven.

CHAPTER FOUR

THE RESURRECTION

I translated back into my body with a force that tore apart the wrappings that supported the body that was once me. The flesh was a decomposing mess. Guess I'll never know why Jesus saw it fit to send me back to occupy it in that state. I suppose answers will be found when we meet again face to face.

"This is a demon," those around screamed, when they noticed what was happening. It was a panic situation rid of order. The whole room was shaken. Very disturbed by my return from the dead, I straitening up and I dusted off the maggots that squirmed all around my ears, mouth and my entire face.

My left hand and left leg were deformed as before. The limbs barely held. I pulled them closer to the rest of my body supporting them

79

all along with the right hand which could function. Awkward as it was I was not in pain.

Eyes stared in shock, wonder and disbelief! "He's a demon ... He's been dead for seven days...," it was a beehive of terrified voices.

I leaned back - watching, hearing, and saying nothing. When I opened my mouth it was to pray and commend the assignment ahead, and my nation to the Lord. Strange, but I had no idea that I was gone for seven days, now that someone mentioned it, it worried me. According to me I was gone for just a few hours.

"Emmanuel, Emmanuel!" a voice called twice. *"You have been dead for 7 days,"* it was Jesus speaking closely. He said that it was impossible to know the length of the seven days in heaven, because there is neither day nor night in heaven. There is no keeping our earthly sense of time. The light of Jesus enlightens heaven, it's simply glorious as they all wait for the day all the saints will dine and be crowned together.

THE WAR IS OVER

Rwanda enjoyed relative calm. The fighting and killing was subsiding promising to bring the cruel war to an end. I had returned from heaven with a message for my nation. Jesus wanted everyone who had made a vow during the fighting to fulfill the promise. The calm atmosphere offered an opportune time for people to keep their word. Christ wanted the Rwandese people to pray and seek for His restoration. He wanted them to know that it was not their guns that had protected them but God. He wanted me to proclaim the message that if they didn't pray and seek God, He would allow a worse scenario to paralyze the country.

For the first time since my return from heaven I spoke to the people around me. I shared about the divine experience, conveying the message Christ had given. Some people ran out screaming. But largely the response was encouraging. Shortly, there was commotion. A contingent of military men swarmed into the room. Apparently the screams from those who ran out fearing me, had drawn the militia men from their hideout. They were shocked to find us alive. According to them everyone in the area had been wiped off in the war.

"How did you escape? How come you were not killed?" a surprised voice asked. "A man in the room was praying for forgiveness. The killers spared our lives when he said he is a Christian," someone answered. "And what are the screams about?" "This man has just resurrected from the dead," someone answered pointing at me. "He says he has been in heaven with Jesus Christ." "He was dead and his body was over there at the corner." A chorus of answers was volunteered.

"Did you see Jesus?" one soldier inquired. "What did He tell you?" All eyes were on me. "Yes, I saw Him," I answered courageously. "He told me to tell you to repent. The war is over but if you won't repent and seek Him, something worse will break out," I continued. The soldiers observed me with obvious interest. Very obviously I had captured their interest. I watched their faces transform as the truth about Jesus Christ registered in softening hardened features. I really wasn't expecting it but one by one the men opened their hearts to receive Jesus Christ. Not all, however, accepted Jesus Christ.

Some of the newly saved soldiers offered to feed us. They left promising to return with our food.

I suppose they went and shared about us because in a while members of the Red Cross arrived ready to move us to a descent camp at Kabwayi in Gitarama province. We were filthy and smelly. Our combined stench was obviously offensive forcing the aides attending to move us to our own room.

Apparently that was not the end of moving. Having been attended to, it was said we should be taken to Nyanza, then to the centre for the disabled at Rilima in Bugesera.

There our wounds were washed and treated. It was common to put the patients to sleep by administering tranquilizers. I never went to sleep on any of these. Although I was in bad shape, i wasn't in pain. I used to intercede for the other patients praying that they would sleep well without being on tranquillizers.

At *King Faycal Hospital* in Kigali we continued receiving treatment. The Red Cross team placed metal insertions in my left hand and leg and plastered them. They did so yet still believing none of the parts was going to mend again, ever. Doctors said I would end up with a lethal infection if the limbs were not amputated. Once after a checkup I was notified I was among the people listed for theatre the following day. "Do not eat anything," was the parting word.

CHAPTER FIVE

DIVINE PROVISION

Desperately, I cried to God reminding Him of His promise to send me all over the world preaching the gospel of Jesus Christ.

"Shall I go without limbs?" I cried. I must have drifted off to sleep at some point of wrestling with God because I had an extremely vivid dream in which a man I recognized as a local businessman was preaching without a leg and a hand.

"He is preaching the gospel without his hand and leg," Jesus commented in the dream. "But he got saved that way," I answered back, "he got saved after the war and he has no account in heaven. I have served You through the years," I bargained. ***"Yes I know,"*** the Lord said. ***"I will not let your hand and leg be cut off. Eat and drink."*** My peace was restored.

The only hitch was that there was no food to eat. ***"I will send you something to eat,"*** came Jesus' rejoinder.

When I awoke up, a man, a complete stranger walked towards me confidently. He placed a plastic bag on a small table near my bed and looked at me. "God has directed me to bring you these," he said pointing at the bag. "It's your food." He left as abruptly as he had entered. The bag contained a packet of milk and a loaf of bread. The brief encounter left me speechless.

The hospital staff was unable to mask their irritation when they showed up at my bed to take me to the theatre, only to find me eating. Angry, they demanded to know why I had defied their instructions. I retorted that God had refused me to be amputated on. They left. I thanked God, trusting that the amputation matter was laid to rest - once and for all.

In the afternoon, a man I once worked with in a German company came to the hospital. We talked at length. I was happy to hear from him that the company was back in full swing, and that the directors were caring for any of their staff maimed during the war.

Seeing my predicament, he promised to follow up the possibility of my receiving specialized treatment overseas - on the company's account. "Please do it as soon as possible, even today," I pleaded. I was desperate. We parted with his promise of some quick action. True to his words he was back later saying that all I needed was a passport to travel to the hospital in Brussels, Belgium. He had even brought a photographer to take my snaps for the document to be processed.

Quite oblivious of my plans, the hospital staff served fresh a notice warning me not to eat. I was due in the theatre again, they insisted. Once again I cried to the Lord reminding Him of my diligent service. The Spirit of the Lord comforted me with the same message, *"Eat and drink, there will be no amputation."*

My breakfast was served miraculously the following morning, again. A stranger walked in, in the now familiar manner carrying my food - exactly five minutes before I was due for theatre.

You can imagine how the hospital crew was enraged. To them I appeared to have lost my mind. My defiance was promptly reported to the senior director.

"We do not play games here." I got the tongue lashing from the senior director a week later. "Tomorrow this hand and leg will be amputated, okay?" he said pointing at the parts. My inward response was a big no! He left as abruptly as he had appeared to fill the space next to me. Alone, I turned to the wall onto my routine combination of crying and praying. Still, I echoed the same persistent reminders of years of faithfulness in God's service.

I talked to God about the people He could use to rescue me from the situation. That night God said, *"I have heard your cry. There will be no amputation; you will preach My Word around the world."*

That next morning breakfast was delivered promptly by the same man who brought it the very first time. Receiving the food from him, I thanked him and began to eat. The senior director was furious when this was reported to him. He ordered the nurses to throw me out of the bed, saying it should be occupied by a more 'serious' patient.

When doctors speak, nurses act - angry hands lifted me in the air dumping me on the cold floor. Jeering and sneering, the nurses told me I wouldn't last long. "Ask the people who bring you food to help you," one of them said, dripping with sarcasm.

I sang to the Lord, oblivious of the mockery. But the staff wouldn't let me be, they bullied me mercilessly. A doctor was put on stand by to tell the people who fed me to take me away. In the course of time, the man who had been feeding me walked in.

Roughly, he was stopped and commanded to carry me out of the hospital. My visitor explained that he wouldn't manage that by himself. He tried to explain that it would require many hands to carry me. I began to pray loudly as I watched the exchange.

"Do you think there is God in Rwanda," the doctor asked rudely when he heard me praying. "Let's see if your God will send you a car," he said sarcastically when he heard me plead with God to send some means of transport. I continued praying, asking God to forgive the man.

"If at all there's God, why did He let so many people die?" he continued in the same rough tone. "There is God in Rwanda. That's why you are still alive and breathing,' I responded. The doctor motioned to some staff to help the man take me outside. The order was obeyed.

The doctor walked ahead, leading us to the spot where I was to be dumped. Just then I noticed a white car driving in. "Please take me to that car," I ordered. The mean looking driver softened up when he saw and assessed what was happening. My entire experience, the past few weeks came out fast as I told him everything. It touched him to say the least and he accepted to drive me home. As he sped off,

I caught a glimpse of the senior doctor watching us from a balcony on the hospital's top floor.

CHAPTER SIX

HOME SWEET HOME

Finally, I was at home laid out on a mat. All along, I had never received proper treatment and my leg and hand were deteriorating owing to this. I was desperate. Desperation is – having all exit routes sealed, and it's you against the world. That describes the man who lay on a mat, waiting for a word to rescue the situation.

Everyday, I hoped for a word from my former colleague or employer. I was expectant, wanting to know whether I was enlisted for treatment in Brussels, Belgium.

As the long hours dragged by, my hopelessness increased – was that it; was it the end? I felt worse by the minute; maggots were gnawing at my wounds.

The nagging thoughts terrified me seeing it was impossible to ever return to the hospital where I was kicked out. 'Maybe it's not such a bad idea to try out the hospital where I was first admitted when I sustained these injuries,' I thought.

I was taken back to the hospital (*Centre Hospitalier de Kigali*), one blue Monday morning. The long queue told of the true state of the Rwandese people. Casualties, all war victims, hit by a bullet, slashed by a machete or certainly injured by a weapon, waited in line for treatment. A nurse walked towards me. Her detailed observation was followed by a sour expression. I understood the look. Every inch of me looked awful, even worse, I smelled foul.

"Are you born again?" she asked, almost sharply.

"Yes."

"A white man from Australia has been asking for a particular man," she went on, her voice adopting a friendlier tone. "He has been sent by God to treat a man with injuries on the left hand, and left leg." I didn't want to celebrate too soon, in case she went on to give attributes that would disqualify the possibility that it was me she talked about.

She went on, "the man we are looking for is scheduled for amputation but God has reversed doctor's diagnosis,"

The Australian had made it plain that the man God sent him to treat would be brought to that particular hospital. At one point, he did begin to get a bit anxious having failed to trace the right person, until God urged him to relax assuring him, he would show up, in due time.

It appeared that the nurse had set out to question new arrivals, until she found the wanted man. Her strategy was simple; first, she wanted to know if the man, for she only questioned men, had an injured left hand, and leg; Next, she'd want to know if the person was saved. So far, no one satisfying the precise details had showed up - until the day she talked to me. Two men she'd thought met the bracket were turned down.

She looked at me over saying that the Australian doctor had a picture of the person sought for. "God has given this man a new name," she volunteered. "But the doctor has not disclosed these to anyone," she carried on referring to the picture and 'new' name privy to the doctor.

She mentioned that the Australian may be interested in seeing me saying she was prepared to take me to verify if I was the wanted man.

'If it is me; If I get healed; If...,' the thoughts, as though suddenly unlocked, like rain drops from the heavens, streamed in steadily. 'I will serve you faithfully; I will never slacken in my faith again." My heart was pounding at the possibilities, the possibility of becoming whole again.

UMWANA W'UMWAMI (CHILD OF THE KING)

"He is the one,' the white man staring at me shouted. His room was in a section reserved for the affluent members of the Rwandese society. With a pocketed hand, the man I'd met for less than a minute scrutinized me. His face radiated the joy one feels on finding a lost object long sought for. An instant surge of energy flowed through me.

"Are you Emmanuel Twagirimana?"

"Yes."

As he reached for his drawer, I watched with bated breath wondering what he was up to. Pulling it open, he picked out a picture of a man and put it before my face. "God has given you a new name. You are now Umwana W'Umwami!"

The picture was a replica of my image, the doctor had hand drawn. Feeling at ease with each other we talked freely. Dr. John Simpson opened up that he doubled as doctor and a military man.

"I specialize in head cases," he said fixing me his keen gaze. "I struggled with God in prayer wondering how to deal with your case. Its only after He assured me, He'd lead the way that I came," he continued in a thick Australian accent."

Dr. Simpson as I came to learn, had traveled to Africa expecting to depend entirely on God's leading, in the treating my complications. Part of the divine instructions required the doctor to graft part of my hip area, onto my damaged arm. He had been told to leave an empty space between the two bones to allow room for marrow development. A similar process outlined by God was to be followed in fixing my leg. He'd have to fit metal insertions.

Post-operation care came strictly from above. God had outlined each step to be adhered to for my healing and recovery; that included every single incision, stitch and everything else meant to bring my good health back on. The full set of equipment required to operate on me cost a whooping $100,000.

"I pray and fast for forty days for God to send me to a particular case. You are the third person He has directed me to." Hearing him talk lulled me into relaxation. Somehow I held the belief that I was in able hands. "There is no cause to fear," He assured over and over, "you will go through all the stages and recover well."

"Have you eaten anything?"

"I had some breakfast,' I replied.

"Please get into prayer and fasting." He told me that he was on his first day of doing the same. "Have the nurse clean your wounds then go home and begin seeking God. We will meet again in three days."

With that we broke company.

THE DIVINE OPERATION

"Take this in your mouth." It was Thursday morning and the doctor held some apparatus close to my lips. Within minutes of taking in the clear fluid, I became drowsy. That's the most I can remember of Thursday, apart from the part when Dr. Simpson shaved off my hairy legs and arms just before the operation.

When I came back to consciousness, I lay in a quiet room. It was Friday. Dr. Simpson sat close by, assuring me it was okay. I needed to eat, he said. He spoon-fed me. From then, I was utterly and completely given to his caring hands. He did everything for me.

He wouldn't take no for an answer in as far as caring for my needs was concerned, "I will get a blessing from doing this for you," he often scolded.

Within three weeks it was evident I had taken well to the operation. Dr. Simpson termed it "successful," and it was obviously so, given the way I felt and looked. The metal inserts fitted in my body with precision.

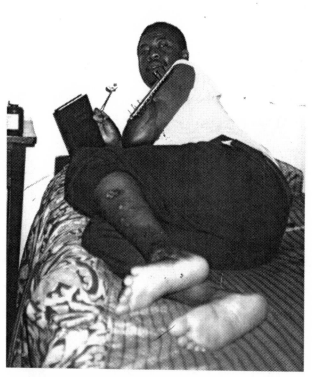

Still recovering from the wound on my foot.

A couple of weeks later, the doctor suggested that I try out a wheelchair, as the next part in the healing process. From then, he would move me about on the wheel chair, allowing me to wheel myself when I could.

That was until he brought a pair of crutches. Dr. Simpson helped about, on the metal props until I found the perfect balance. Together we learnt the art of walking on the crutches.

By the day, aided by the bighearted Godsend gentleman from way yonder - I evolved into a brand new person. Dr. Simpson even picked me out a new wardrobe, complete with a pair of shoes. "I bought these by faith," he said pointing at the shoes, "because I believe you will walk again."

There was a bond between us. A close friendship fostered and seasoned by frequent moments of prayer. The presence was so real in our friendship. He showed Himself to us in a wonderful way, talking to us about great mysteries.

A NEW PREACHER

I walked back to the home I had left a month earlier a new creature, a new man. I was a new person, having been overhauled in every aspect. The day I was taken back to my house, we spent the night there with my doctor friend.

He chose a spot on the floor where he spent praising and thanking God through the night. He was overjoyed by the successful mission.

The day before he left, he prayed for me laying hands on me and anointed me. He commissioned me to go out and serve the Lord. He left some drugs and bandages behind and gave me instructions on how to care for myself as I recuperated.

CHAPTER SEVEN

TIME TO INVEST

God invests in our lives expecting not just a harvest, but a bumper harvest in return. God's every move is a well-thought plan, with the potential to succeed. This is so clear in many verses in the Bible. Take for example the parable of the talents in which, the master gives out; five talents to one man, two to another and one talent to the third servant. Trusting that the talents will be multiplied, the master packs his bags and goes away on safari.

On his return, the master receives joyously the servant with five talents for doubling them, the same, to the man who was given two talents. He is rewarded for duplicating his two into four. The third servant, given one talent is severely rebuked giving unacceptable excuses and exaggerations, about why he couldn't multiply the talent. This man is cast into the pit where there is gnashing of teeth and continual crying. God is interested in our increase. As the master who was pleased with and rewarded the servants who had taken what he'd entrusted them with to next level, God rejoices in you when you multiply what He has entrusted you with.

God invested a lot in me. When the time came to take every investment to the next level - I did exactly that. I began preaching with metal insertions still on me; sometimes in pain and many times in want. I have been rejected, misunderstood, and have slept in dingy places - but yet- I have continued on the long winding road.

RWANDA

I started the work of God in my native country, preaching about Jesus and giving His message. Many gave their lives to The Lord. However, Rwanda was not easy. A cloud of doubt, thickened by tribal animosity and supported by unforgiveness, made it difficult to talk about Jesus. People opposed the gospel openly. They questioned how a God so good, would have allowed such calamity; or why they should forgive those who'd murdered their fathers, uncles, spouses etc.

Sometimes it was beyond me to provide adequate answers, without the Holy Spirit's intervention. Also when the going got too tough, God released His ministering angels to watch over me; I sensed their presence many times.

I knew that Jesus Christ wanted me to persist, until the strongholds gave way. I have been to every province in Rwanda proclaiming; forgiveness, repentance and a fresh beginning.

DEMOCRATIC REPUBLIC OF CONGO

At the DRC, a doctor who'd heard that a good number of staffs at his hospital got saved at my crusade at Kinshasa was not at all amused. He openly challenged my story saying it beat logic how a man could die and come back to life. And in that fashion, he raised fierce arguments insisting I hadn't died - but was in a coma for 7 days.

Preaching showing my injured arm.

"Let that God who resurrected you, make me blind- then maybe, just maybe I'll believe in Him!" he challenged. His wish was granted – instantly, his sight disappeared. No hospital could reverse the sight God had taken. And so the doctor agonized in total darkness.

Three days of blindness were all he could take for. He duly sent word to my hotel, saying "he needed prayers.' I went to him. He was broken and ready to accept Jesus Christ. I prayed and his sight was restored. He later was called in fulltime ministry.

TANZANIA

I had a very interesting experience once in Tanzania. I couldn't afford to put up at a hotel, and so, God directed me to go to sleep in a nearby bush. He wanted me to pray for the great work ahead. I obeyed. I interceded for the town, Biharamulu town, demolishing strongholds, and calling the folk there to salvation. I drifted off to sleep, only to be woken by drops of water – it was raining. God must have had His own special reason, for having me out there unsheltered from the rain. After a while the rain subsided and I drifted off to sleep, I heard a movement in the thicket, it was too dark to see anything – except the two golden eyes that advanced stealthily – it was a leopard.

Fear griped me. I couldn't move neither scream, I could do nothing!

Just then, my spirit man came alive with the words, "fear not." God gave me the word in **Genesis 28:15** *"Behold, I am with you and will keep you wherever you go, and will bring you back to this land; for I will not leave you, until I have done what I have spoken to you."*

Again, the Holy Spirit commanded me, ***"Roar like a lion."*** I did just that, producing a roar-like sound that sent the leopard scampering. That's when I was able to laugh.

MWANZA, TANZANIA

Here, two people I prayed for came back to life. One was a three year old baby girl, who'd died in her mother's arms on their way to hospital. I was out for a mission when I encountered the stricken mother. I asked her and her companion why they were crying. They showed me the baby's body. I held the dead baby in my arms and prayed for a fresh lease of life. The little life was restored. I gave the baby back to her mother and told them "go back the baby is whole" they went back home.

The next was a young bachelor called Innocent. I'd met his two sisters earlier and requested them to look for me where I would stay. They agreed to host me briefly at their parent's home. As I shared my testimony with the parents it really interested them, given that their son lay sick in hospital. I was left interceding for the boy when his sisters left the next day to see him at the hospital. God gave me the word from **John 11: 4** *"This sickness is not unto death, but for the glory of God..."*

When I accompanied them the next day, we found that he'd deteriorated overnight; He was dying. A voice kept urging me to assure them that their son, and brother would live, but I panicked at the thought of it. Finally I did. Sure enough, Innocent opened his eyes and smiled. It was such a relief, and we were excited about it. The two girls prompted informed their parents of everything. Their mother accepted

Jesus Christ, but their father said that he would have to see his son first to decide.

The next morning, we were told that Innocent had died in the night, and his remains moved to the morgue. Boy, we were shocked! I had to take control of the situation somehow to restore the family's confidence in God. "Make no plans for burial yet," I broke in; "bring Innocent's body here." And so, Innocent now several hours dead, and as cold as a grave, was brought home. I prayed that whole day without a change. The following and the next, I spent in, holed up in prayer.

On the third day I saw a dream in which I stretched out on the dead body, breathing into its nostrils. He came back to life, and offered him a drink from a glass. I woke up shaking. Not too long after, God commanded me to go and do exactly as it was in the dream. The body was by then days old, and I wasn't excited at all about touching it, let alone lying on top of it - worse still breathing into it. I told God that I couldn't do it. God insisted. I obeyed. I never wanted to anger God. As in the dream, I lay on top of the body and breathed into the nostrils – the dead came back to life. Innocent opened his eyes slowly at first, then fully. I opened the door to call his family to come, a multitude of people had come to see what would happen, when they saw him, they ran, screaming.

We helped him to sit up, and gave him some fresh juice.

I continued to preach, and many people gave their lives to Christ. There was a wealthy man who gave his life to Christ but his friends were not happy. One of his friends brought me millions of Tanzanian shillings and two cars.

He pleaded with me to leave that area and never preach Christ again. I refused. Furious, he left without adding any more word. I was kidnapped that evening by a speeding car without registration number as another Pastor and I were waiting for the Pastor's driver to pick us.

Three men came out of that car and suddenly hit the pastor then threw me into the car.

An hour later, we reached a place where they threw me in a small, dirty house. At around 2 am I fell asleep and had a dream; I saw people coming to kill me. I woke up and started to pray. One hour later, I heard somebody trying to open my door. I prayed and prayed loudly, God brought a strong wind which shook the roof of that small house, a lot of dust brought by the wind disturbed them and they ran away.

Come morning, they came back and said "Do not pray, we just want to open for you" They opened and told me to leave .I refused and started to preach to them. To my surprise they all received the gospel and accepted Jesus Christ and were saved.

They later confessed that they had come to kill me and bury me there. They went on to show me where my grave was already dug. "We were sent by that man who tried to bribe you" they then told me.

When he heard that I was not killed, he fled to Dar es Salaam.

His four wives were saved when I went to see them and preached to them. Three of them left, they could not continue living with him as his wives. His very first wife was the one who remained in their home. Months after this man too received Christ

SOUTH AFRICA

At a crusade, among other miracles, I got an opportunity to pray for a respected personality who was instantly healed of cancer.

BOMBAY- INDIA

The Holy Spirit came over me so strongly, that I preached in Hindu language since I did not have an interpreter. About five thousand people gave their lives to Christ in that crusade.

OXFORD-ENGLAND

Many were healed of HIV/AIDS and other chronic ailments in various meetings I held there. A member of a notable family also invited me to talk to her more about God's healing power.

AIRBORNE, EGYPT AIR

The experience in mid-air was quite something. This was back in 1999, as I traveled back home aboard an Egypt Air aircraft. All began well, actually on a high note, as I shared my life's story with the passengers who cared to listen. Most ignored the 'fairytale' others just engaged me in theological arguments. It was on that note that the pilot's voice broke through to announce a mechanical hitch in the plane. It was very serious, and lives were at risk, one of the cabin crew divulged, she said the engine had failed.

The crash-scare went round very quickly, and people were on panic-mode. I seized that as the perfect moment to talk about the message of salvation. At one point, the plane stopped moving altogether. I believe that the Lord supported the plane in that instant. People paid attention then, and I prayed for anyone who wished, leading many, especially the crews to salvation. Then, I prayed for God to reverse the situation - the engine roared back into life. Two hours later we checked in at Cairo Airport. That was another opportunity to proclaim Jesus Christ. More people gave their lives to Christ.

In 2001, during a stop over at Cairo Airport while en route to England, an airport office that had got saved in the episode, 2 years before, recognized me. He convinced me to meet with some of his brethren. "**Go**," God said, "**I have work for you to do here**." I was told to preach on that same day.

Next day, I called for baptism. We went to a close by river and, duly began the process. A crippled man, who'd been saved the previous day, stepped forward for baptism. I plunged him in the water in the usual way only for him to emerge totally healed. Glory to God! Not only was he healed, but he spoke in new tongues – praise the Lord again!

The whole event attracted a crowd, most of who were met with the power of the Holy Spirit and got saved and baptized.

ITALY

A trip to Italy provided the opportunity to meet with high ranking leaders of the Catholic Church. We shared at length on various subjects. When the perfect moment presented itself, I told them about my death-and-back-to-life-experience.

HEALING

While in a convention in **Washington DC** in 1998, my leg developed extreme pain. I prayed about it, but the pain wouldn't ease. The Holy Spirit drew my attention to the metal insertions therein, saying it was time to have them removed. I checked into a small hospital where an operation to take out the bits went on successfully. The leg however, developed a life-sized wound that needed delicate daily care. I had to continue walking with a crutch.

I was in **the United Kingdom** in 1999. During a prayer session, God instructed me to go and have the metal fittings in my arm removed. At one of Oxford Radcliffe Hospitals, the doctor wanted to know if I had a special letter from my doctor or any hospital transfer from my country. I had none. I simply explained that I was there on divine business. He seemed to understand that bit and consequently proceeded to carry out the minor operation. Three days later, my hand was good and well.

I then continued to walk with the help of a crutch. I could not make any single step without it; my leg was not fully healed.

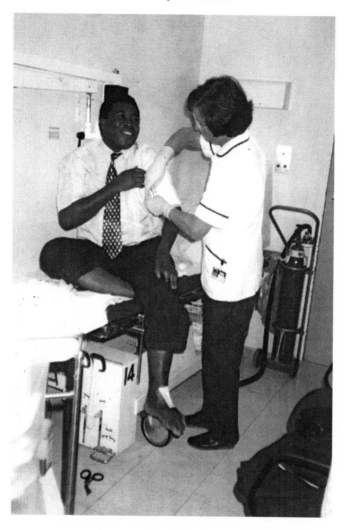

Just removed the metal supports from my arm in England.

CHAPTER EIGHT

WEDDING BELLS

Isabelle and I on our wedding day.

Before I traveled to the United States in 1998, I went before the Lord praying for my trip and the work that I had to do there. God answered my prayer, I preached in some cities of the United States, and Canada. Miracles of healing and deliverance took place. When I came back home, I straight away went into thanksgiving fasting prayer.

God told me *"Many people come before me to ask of me, you have come give thanks; I am going to give you something very special. Look I am preparing your bride and you will wed on July 7, 2001"*

Then God showed her to me in a vision and revealed her name to me. I started preparations of the wedding when I came back from Sweden in 2000, the first committee which would be in charge of planning the day sat before I had ever physically met my bride to be. This was in response to God's voice and promise.

The year 2000, found me preaching to some young people in Nairobi, Kenya. God sent me there with a word to bless and direct their youth. That's when I saw her for the first time – my promised bride. No one needed to confirm that I was looking at the woman who would be - my wife; my life partner.

God had showed her to me in a vision; her names and wedding date, July 7, 2001 included.

Isabelle was leading the service. No doubt she caught my eye that first day, as it has continued to this very day. She stood at the pulpit with a dignified air about her, the Holy Spirit's anointing clearly evident as she paced about gracefully. I sat down smiling boyishly, mesmerized by the woman who stood before us so confidently. The Holy Spirit's whisper that I have learnt to expect at any moment reached in me that dazed moment; *"you are looking at the woman that I have prepared for you.'* That only widened the boyish grin. I remember her throwing a quick glance my way, not an interested look, just one of those that mean.

From then, I had to fight to fix my thoughts, as well as my attention on the sermon I was expected to deliver shortly. With effort, that was possible and when my name was announced, I was composed enough as I took position behind the glass podium. I left shortly after the service.

Days later, Isabelle and I met face to face – for the first time. I felt that I should take that chance to propose to her, but restrained myself. Progressively we cultivated a deep friendship, which led to courtship. Later, I proposed, not on the proverbial bended knee, but at least I scored high for she said - yes. As they say the rest is history.

God had said that on my wedding day I would walk down the aisle - as any eager bridegroom – without a crutch. Wherever I went, I spread that message. Still, many days passed by without any sign that I'd recover.

A week before the wedding, friends suggested that I ought to cancel the wedding. They were providing what they thought were 'safe' alternatives, to avoid my biggest embarrassment on my wedding day, since I had not healed. I would not have it. Come July 6, with a crutch still under my arm, with evidence of things not seen-my healing, I was up and about so much during the day and my leg hurt terribly. Night fell, and I crawled into bed, still anticipating God's healing.

That night, I had the most extraordinary dream. In it, - I was stretched out on a bed, inside what appeared to be a theatre room of a remarkably clean hospital. Three doctors stood by my side. One introduced himself as an angel-doctor saying, *"I have been sent by Jesus Christ to heal you, because of your wedding this morning."*

I remember being so worried about the procedure, because I never wanted anything to spoil what lay ahead, but was gently reassured that everything was in good hands, and that after I would look better for my wedding day.

With that, the angel-doctor picked my bad leg in his hand gave a soft tag. He then rubbed it down gently, giving a slow massage down to the sole area - that instantaneously sparked off a healing process, which I could literally feel coming in. Shortly, we were back in my bedroom.

I was asked to put on some socks and shoes, and to toss the crutch through the window of our third-floor apartment. I did just that, and began walking to the gate as instructed. At first it was a step, then a hop and a leap and then it was a song HALLELUJAH, followed by shouts of joy. I was overwhelmed. In the same manner, I skipped back to the house, and tucked in sleep. I jolted from sleep to realize I was enjoying a good dream.

Right then, God spoke to me saying, *"I have healed you. Get up and do what you did in the dream."* I got up instantly, however, the thought of walking on my sick leg without a crutch, terrified me. I leaned against the wall hesitantly, not able to take the risk. *"Do not fear you are already healed."* I like Peter's attempt to walk on water, summoned on by the Saviour's call - I stepped out in faith. One step, then another until, just like in the dream it was a happy trot. Oh! What a Miracle. I walked out of the house towards the gate, praising God. Mind you this was at 3am.

God is not a man that He should lie. **Numbers 23:19**

People surprised me by saying that none had heard my little dance of joy the previous night.

The house was crammed-full, surely I had woken up someone. No one! And for I was the centre of attention as people asked to be told narrate my dream over and over again. I had to remind them that I had a bride to marry that morning.

I married Isabelle on July 7th. 2001. Our wedding was solemnized at Redeemed Gospel Church, officiated by my mentor Bishop Dr. Arthur Kitonga.

Ordination day with Bishop Dr. Arthur Kitonga

My family: (From left) Jemima, myself, Isabelle and Joshua.

As I write this, I marvel at her tireless dedication to see this book, and other things we have planned come to pass. She has typed and re-typed as well as read through the manuscripts patiently – truly God is a matchmaker.

Step by step, God has potted us into best friends. It's not always a rosy affair, challenges do come, as they will continue to, but we have learnt to allow the ongoing process that is growth and maturity happen.

FORGIVENESS

Therefore if your enemy is hungry, feed him; if he is thirsty, give him a drink: for in so doing you will heap coals of fire on his head. Do not be overcome by evil, but overcome evil with good. **Romans 12:20-21**

Then Peter came to Him and said, "Lord how often shall my brother sin against me, and I forgive him? Up to seven times?" Jesus said to him, "I do not say to you, up to seven times: but up to seventy times seven. **Mat 18: 21-22.**

I returned to my country for a visit after my wedding, I met a man who'd really frustrated me while I was very sick. He did not believe it when I popped up in his office unannounced. He stared in disbelief.

"Can you remember me?" I asked him.

"You look like a man who used to be called Emmanuel Twagirimana."

"I am Emmanuel!"

131

"That cannot be; it's impossible!" He simply did not believe it. I moved closer to reveal the scars, left to convince doubting Thomas. Slowly he removed rimmed spectacles, and with a slight squint proceeded to scrutinize the unveiled marks. Unexpectedly, he burst into tears. He was convinced; and convicted.

"Remember what you said," I prodded. "That if I got healed you would surrender your life to Christ, well this is the time," I challenged. Right there and right then he received Jesus Christ. I laid my hands on him and prayed. Now a believer he sunk to the floor overcome by the power of God. He was crying all the time.

A while later; we walked side by side, to the parking lot. Incidentally, his car was parked next to mine. A small tap on the window, stopped me just as I was about to drive off. The man had something further to say. The confession came slowly. I received it graciously. "I know I'm now a believer, but will God really forgive me?" "Yes, yes," I assured. He asked whether I had forgiven

132

him, to which he was assured positively. We embraced warmly. He was free. He looked free.

We must forgive unconditionally. Yes, forgiving is no easy task, still we must learn how to, if we want to please God. Unforgiveness can hinder someone to inherit the eternal life. By praying for our enemies, God insures that they live long to witness the blessing of the Lord in our lives, those that they wished we wouldn't have. That way their hearts are won to Christ.

PLEASE STAND UP

As said in my Introduction, the world is forcing down our throats distorted images, opinions, beliefs, and so much more on what the future holds. They want you to believe that Christ is never returning for a spotless bride.

That's why it is extremely important that you and I stand up to be counted among God's end-time generals. Simply because the Truth lives in us and He has saved us, we qualify to become the solution to a world that is bouncing back and forth in a violent-flow river with no exit route. We should stand up and become the fishers-of-men, to steer the boat back to sanity.

In the last couple of months I have become more convinced that we are seeing the sunset of events on earth. Please stand up and respond to God's cry to save souls. Please stand up and position yourself to save souls.

I'll say this - the most unfortunate thing that can ever happen to you is not to be deserted by a close friend, or to be dismissed from the job. The most unfortunate thing is when, you are too fear-stricken to go dislodge from the world's grip and become the end-time General God wants you to be. The courage to tread into deeper waters and into new lands defines the soul-winners, from mark timers. Soul-winners, or fishers-of-men or, end time Generals, whichever you prefer, will see the giants in the land, yet step in to possess it.

You don't have to have died, and resurrected for God to use you greatly, as simple as your testimony is – God wants to use you.

Isabelle and I are praying for you.

Author Information

As a crusade and conference speaker whom God has raised up as a prophetic voice, REV EMMANUEL TWAGIRIMANA calls people to Christ. He teaches about FAITH and LOVE and leaves you with the knowledge that transforms your life. He and his wife Isabelle have two children Joshua and Jemima.

To have Rev Emmanuel Twagirimana at your next event, call:
+254 722217710

Email at
nlgc777@yahoo.com
newlife@7daysinheaven.org

Please visit our website at
www.7daysinheaven.org

CPSIA information can be obtained at www.ICGtesting.com
Printed in the USA
236337LV00001B/77/A